Book Design: Andro Bottros

ST SHENOUDA PRESS
8419 Putty Rd,
Putty, NSW, 2330
Sydney, Australia

www.stshenoudapress.com

ISBN: 978-0-6482814-8-1

Anna Simone was one of the royal children of the King of Constantinople. Her mother past away when she was young, and so I was asked by the King to look after her. As a priest, it was my duty to show her the way of life which is pleasing to God, as found in the Bible. I often read her the stories of saintly monks, nuns and hermits, explaining that these people lived that way because of their great love for God. She admired their stories, especially how little they ate and how much time they spent in prayer and quiet contemplation.

In fact, she loved to borrow my books and read the stories of the saints repeatedly. I would constantly find her sitting in a quiet area of the castle reading, both during the day and night. It soon became obvious that she preferred such spiritual time even over all the glamour and ceremonies of the royal family's life. I also noticed when there were large feasts and celebrations, that she wouldn't eat of the food. Such food would be cooked by the very best chefs throughout the land, but she still would not have a single bite.

One night, as I walked down the corridor, I heard the sound of crying. As I listened more closely, it was coming from Anna Simone's chamber. Worried that something had happened to her, I peeked through the keyhole and saw her sobbing indeed, with her eyes and arms lifted towards Heaven.

I stood there for a while to listen. She began to pray, "My Lord, You alone know the secrets of my heart. Please help me to do Your Will. I have now read all about the saintly hermits, under the guidance of my spiritual father the

3

priest. If it is Your Will, I desire to live like them. I want to go somewhere else and live a life of serving You."

As I heard these words, I became greatly worried, yet extremely joyful at the same time! I began to fear her father's reaction if he found out that Anna Simone wants to leave the palace. Yet on the other hand, I thanked God deeply for her spiritual zeal and her desire to live for the Lord, despite her young age. But when was she planning on leaving?

Just as I was about to leave, she shocked me with the next thing she did. I continued to watch her through the keyhole. To my surprise, she pulled out a bag of food from beneath her bed, and began dividing the food into smaller bags.

That explained everything! I knew that there was something behind her recent choice of eating dry bread and salty cheese every day. I figured that instead of eating herself, she would gather the food from the palace and give it away freely to the poor. She did all this in secret, without anyone seeing or praising her

good deeds. She reminded me of the Lord's teaching in Matthew 6:1, "Take heed that you do not do your charitable deeds before men, to be seen by them."

It was then that I heard her pray, "Dearest Heavenly Father, I desire to serve my brothers and sisters who are less fortunate than I. These people have no food or shelter. Please look after them, Lord. I will give them my food. As for myself, all I want is to live with You and for You. Amen."

Several years past and the King died, leaving Anna Simone as the next person to inherit the throne. The morning on which she was to be crowned Queen, I was sitting with her in the palace. "I will never forget the valuable lessons you taught me all my life, father." She began telling me. "Please continue telling me about this saint you were just mentioning ..."

Before she could continue, her words were interrupted and the army commander called for her. Upon entering the courtyard, there were enormously large crowds gathering from every direction.

The Patriarch, bishops and other priests were also present. Suddenly, there was silence... the commander brought Anna Simone out on the balcony overlooking the courtyard.

"I now crown you, Queen Anna Simone, ruler of Constantinople. Long live the Queen!" the commander shouted. A little boy nearby could not help but yell, "She gave me food when I had nothing to eat!" Then another young mother also cried out, "Yes, she is the one who sent milk and a warm blanket for my newborn!" The people immediately began singing and cheering in celebration of their new Queen.

8

"Long live the Queen!" the crowd shouted repeatedly. The people rejoiced, "Blessed is He* who comes in the name of the Lord! How blessed we are to have a queen who loves the Lord and in turn loves us very much."

There was peace and happiness throughout the entire kingdom. She would let all the captives in jail go free and provide shelter to the homeless. I would often also hear her directing messengers to distribute money and possessions to the neighboring monasteries, to the widows, the orphans and to all the poor who lived in the kingdom. And through this all, she would pray.

However, I could see on Queen Anna Simone's face that this honour she was receiving was not what she wanted. It was obvious that her mind was still occupied with living entirely for the Lord.

She had everything any person would dream of, riches, fame and power, but all this did not satisfy her. One of her favourite verses growing up was, "For what will it profit a man if he gains the whole world, and loses his own soul?" (Mark 8:36)

There was one night that I will never forget. I was lighting some candles throughout the castle, and as I walked past Queen Anna Simone's chamber, I heard her talking out loud to herself.

"Don't you realise that the Lord Jesus Christ has given you so many blessings and gifts? You have fulfilled your life here enough. If you want to attain the Kingdom of Heaven, then now is the time. Remember the Scriptures. Whoever does not carry his cross ..."

I found myself saying the words too, "Whoever does not carry his cross and follow **Me**, is not worthy of **Me**." It was then that I knew what she was going to do. She placed her crown on the throne and bowed in prayer. "I leave this kingdom now because of my love for the Lord Jesus Christ," she added.

She dressed herself in the clothes of a servant and covered her head. I saw her also pick up her Bible and her favourite book, the one about the lives of the saintly hermits. I quickly hid in a dark corner, as she then ran out the palace.

I crept outside and crouched in the shadows of the trees. With her arms
raised to the sky, she thanked God and prayed, "Guide me Lord according to
Your will." Looking at the castle one last time, she asked God to take care of
the kingdom, made the sign of the cross, and headed towards the wilderness.

I was very worried for her. She was walking towards the wilderness during
the night! How would she protect herself and stay warm? Surely her bare feet
would bleed from the rough paths of the wilderness. But, then again, wasn't I

the priest who taught her that the Lord always protects His children? Surely
God won't leave her. He is able to make bitter grass taste like honey for her to
eat. He is able to help her find sweet dates on palm trees. He is able to tame
the wild beasts such that they would become her friends.

I cried knowing it would be unlikely that I would see her ever again. My
comfort, however, was that she was on the path to the Kingdom of Heaven.

It would be several years later that I would hear she was discovered by the
gatekeeper of a faraway convent. I was overjoyed at the news! When the nuns
approached her, she pretended to be crazy. She did this in order to remain
humble and not have her identity as Queen revealed.

Not knowing who she was or what to do with her, The nuns gave her all sorts
of difficult tasks like cleaning the bathrooms and scrubbing the floor. She did
so, however, with great enthusiasm. The nuns were very concerned about her,

because she always chose to sleep on the floor and ate very little.

That was the last I heard of Anna Simone until a visiting monk, Fr Daniel of Scetis, came to my church one day. He spoke to me of a very spiritual girl he had seen. I knew it must have been Anna Simone.

He told me that the Lord Jesus Christ had spoken to him about her, praising her high level of spirituality.

"Anna Simone is a great saint," the Lord told Fr Daniel the monk. "She left her kingdom and now humbles herself as a crazy girl at a convent. Go and see her there."

Fr Daniel the monk then immediately began his journey to the convent. He wanted to go take the blessing of Anna Simone as the Lord told him to. The nuns, however, quickly ran out to him and cried, "Father, keep away from her. She is crazy!"

He replied, "No, she isn't crazy! I see a crown of light upon her head and a
heavenly garment on her body. Open your eyes. Do you not see for yourself?
This is the great Queen Anna Simone. There is no one as pure as her."

Upon hearing this, the nuns wept and fell at Anna Simone's feet pleading,
"Forgive us! Please forgive us!" They kept apologising to her long into the night.
Her identity was revealed, meaning that she would now begin receiving the
honour she tried to escape from in the first place. Since she only desired her
praise to be from the Lord, she left the convent before dawn the next morning.

Just as I was listening to Fr Daniel the monk telling me what else happened to the former Queen, another priest, called Fr John, spoke up, "Let me tell you what I know about Anna Simone."

It was Fr John's last day on earth before passing away. "I was told that only on this day could I tell everyone of what I have seen." said Fr John.

According to Fr John, he was at church early in the morning one day, preparing for the liturgy. All of a sudden, a hermit appeared in the sanctuary

without walking through the church. Fr John was terrified! The hermit asked him for some wine and flour in order to make Holy Bread for the Covenant Thursday liturgy. This was to be celebrated by another 400 hermits. Fr John was very eager to ask where this unknown liturgy was being held.

He then begged him to let him come along. However, the hermit replied, "Wait. Your time will come. Be here at the same time on the same day next year. I will come for you."

The following year, as Fr John was anxiously waiting for the hermit to arrive, he suddenly appeared again in the sanctuary. He asked, "Would you like to see the other hermits?" To this Fr John quickly replied, "I would love to! But before we go father, may I ask, who are the hermits?"

"Son, the hermits are those that live away from anyone else so that they may live alone with God. They leave their families and their friends, and live in a cave in the wilderness so that they can spend all their time with

Jesus Christ. They live there both in the cold and heat and without food storage. They completely depend on God to feed them and provide for their needs. These people live like angels on earth. Come, let us meet them."

He told him to hold onto his garment tightly and to make the sign of the cross. Unexpectedly, there were sounds of mighty winds and crashing waves which frightened Fr John very much. However, when they arrived, Fr John said that he saw beauty that he never witnessed before.

Fr John looked around and found himself in a church he had never seen before. He felt like he was in Heaven while praying with all the hermits. Strangely, he noticed a luminous old lady standing near the front of the church.

After celebrating the Holy Liturgy and receiving communion, he turned to one of the hermit fathers and asked, "Father, who is that blessed old lady standing over there?" he said as he pointed. The lady was being held up by two others.

He looked at him and answered, "Brother, this is Saint Anna Simone, the former queen. But she left the palace to seek the Lord. She is the spiritual guardian of all 400 of us." The hermit told Fr John many more things about her blessed life.

I was very thankful that the Lord sent me Fr Daniel and Fr John to tell me about what they saw of the former queen and great saint, Anna Simone. She loved reading the stories of the saints with me when she was young, and then became a holy saint herself!

CPSIA information can be obtained
at www.ICGtesting.com
Printed in the USA
BVHW022048111020
590798BV00002B/11